I0503130

© SHERYL SPANIER AND KAREN OTAZO 2009

All rights reserved. No part of the book may be reproduced or transmitted in any form or by any means, electronic or mechanical, including photo-copying, recording or by any information storage or retrieval system, without the written permission of the publisher, except where permitted by law.

Published by Sheryl Spanier and Karen Otazo

ISBN 978-1441413758

www.sherylspanier.com

www.global-leadership-network.com

www.notime4theories.com

Author portraits: Ian Spanier
Editor: Nick Kolakowski
Graphic Designer: Mike Bain

Leave Happy

Making the Elegant Executive Transition

BY SHERYL SPANIER AND KAREN OTAZO

Contents

INTRODUCTION: TOMORROW'S WORK CAN WORK FOR YOU

"I've been sold down the river many times and each time to my advantage." — H. L. MENCKEN

First, the bad news: There's been a lot of chatter lately about companies dumping their executives.

With economies and industries in flux, the ensuing career disruptions and executive transitions have become a regular fact of life. We read every day about yet another leave-taking...often accompanied by the negative quotes and narratives of executives desperately fighting change.

Leaders who built and grew their organizations have been given "the boot," and leave feeling undervalued, overlooked and generally abused. After all their years of blood, sweat and tears, it seemed like nobody cared in the end.

You can love a job, but it doesn't love you back.

Now the good news: You can make transitions work for you by refining your view of the workplace, and your place in it.

You can distinguish yourself from those colleagues you read about daily. Being "in transition" is no longer a euphemism for outplacement—organizations, industries, economies, governments and even the environment are expected to remain in continual change and churn. This perpetual "in transition" state will involve arriving, departing and starting anew numerous times during your career. It will be full of both victories and disappointments.

Change your viewpoint, expectations and previous ideas about career success and stability, and you will learn to...

Leave Happy.

If you are:
- In a career transition (or anticipating one)
- Leading an organization in transition
- Trying to gain more control in your career

Then this guide is for you.

Leave Happy is about being happy in the present—whether you're looking to move up, move out or respond to a crisis. It's about using what makes you happy to do whatever you want to do next—and when you're feeling good, you'll find that others will gravitate toward you and want to be a part of your success.

From En-Titled to Emancipated

To Leave Happy (and to be happy at work before you leave), the first step is to realize that your role, title and organization are really vehicles to your professional success—not your identity. Once you shift your view of how to manage your career, you will be ready to enjoy your entry into what we'll call the Post-Millennium Workplace.

With each passing month, the sheer speed of information makes everything increasingly fluid. Companies and contractors can operate anywhere in the world at will; situations can change in the microsecond it takes to email an Excel sheet from Nepal to San Francisco. New and faster media are changing how we see and process the world around us, and as a result we work in ways radically different than we did even five years ago.

In this emerging paradigm, think of your employment as work for hire: The company pays you for your contributions by providing compensation, professional development and interesting assignments—and owes you nothing beyond that. Instead, your professional skills, value and achievements are all 100 percent yours. Creating a new product, solving a problem, innovating, or maximizing financial results are individual successes to be kept in your own experience portfolio.

This "free agent" way of thinking is ever more important, as Job Security becomes an anachronism, and turnover within organizations inevitable. With the right preparation, though, you can shift your thinking from Job Security to Work Continuity.

Master Rolling Transitions

Nothing is going to go back to the way it was. And everything is up for grabs. That's the dark side to this technologically sophisticated, constantly changing Post-Millennium Workplace. As companies move around the globe, acquire, go public and split off, previously secure work environments have transformed into hyper-paced and insecure dwellings for the "working wounded"—executives and their teams who feel victimized by massive economic shifts. More and more senior executives have found diminishing returns in attaching themselves to an organization that dictates their income, deliverables, social status, and leisure time—and makes unilateral decisions without including their perspectives and opinions.

In other words, stability and predictability, or even workplace control, have become past-tense. Instead, recognize that the way to Post-Millennium work and transition happiness lies in mastering the expectations, methods and rules of this new working world— and letting go of resistance to and resentment of the dramatic changes around you.

Traditional methods of doing business have been eroding—and with them, much of the security that once came with working for a big organization. Those leaders who cling to what was, or wait until the marketplace returns to "normal," will stultify talented staff and be unable to compete in the swift, nimble and dynamic future. Even as this scenario plays out on the global stage, the only constant that remains is you: your expertise and experience, reputation and relationships, and guts and grit.

These leadership attributes are needed to succeed in this new environment. Embrace them and you can be more flexible, resilient, innovative, confident and calm. You'll be ready to Leave Happy, long before the departure actually happens. Through becoming someone internally driven—instead of externally manipulated—you'll find more meaning and control in your life and work.

So get ready. As the marketplace shifts, the economy explodes or implodes, and your career becomes one of rolling transitions, the only real control you'll have is your ability to redefine and refine your professional self. In return, though, you'll have the ability to clearly articulate and pursue what you want to do and what you can do, as well as negotiate how much it's worth to the organizations or customers you serve. And that's a recipe for career freedom, pure and simple.

TRADITIONAL WORK MODEL	EMERGENT WORK MODEL
Careers are company-centric	Careers are self-managed
Stability	Shifts
Move up	Move around
Get promoted	Promote yourself
Do it all	Get it done
Find a job that supports your lifestyle	Create work worth

When the Transition Actually Happens

Just as you tend not to dwell on your own mortality unless confronted by it in a physical way, you most likely don't dwell on the "death" of your current job, at least until that position gets "sick," such as when there's a shake-up, or you receive a major professional downer.

Such occurrences may come as a major shock to the system. After all, you've made all the right moves to reach this point: the best schools, strong career track, good reputation, face time. If you remain in your current position, you may start to question its future and your management's strategy/vision; and inevitably, find yourself thinking about either changing the organization or leaving for the competition. If you're on your way out, you desire to re-establish your career as soon as possible—and in a better situation than the one you're leaving. In either case, it's natural to want to regain the position, power, prestige and perks for which you worked so hard.

What Leaving Really Means

Take a moment and imagine yourself on the first day

of your transition. You're standing in your office, and as you slip your service awards and picture frames into that cardboard box, you might feel like you're packing away your very identity along with that bric-a-brac. You might even wonder: Who am I now?

There's only one answer to that, and it's the best possible one: You're still you. You might be leaving behind a position, but that doesn't mean you're leaving your very self along with it.

When you work for an organization, it's easy to sublimate your identity, personality and sense of purpose into the collective. The company has given you a title (identity), a workplace (belonging), purpose (strategy and goals) and a legacy (your results and successes). When you achieve within the company, you advance—and when you leave, it's tempting to believe that you've left all those achievements behind. With that feeling of loss can come a sense of failure or humiliation.

Resist Your First Impulses

Transitions can be protracted or abrupt. Your leave-taking may be imminent or far in the future—or you may be one of the "survivors" who remains in a much-changed organization. No matter what your situation, you might initially develop a wait-and-see attitude, or even become frozen under these conditions; but sooner or later you will want to take charge and move beyond this limbo state as quickly as possible.

So you might:
- Negotiate better terms for yourself, bargain for more time, seek to regain power, and focus on regaining what you are losing
- Write several versions of your resume to suit different positions, either in private business or public service
- Network, hoping someone will know of another job for you, internally or externally
- Look at job ads to replace what you've lost
- Call recruiters, assuming they will have many opportunities for you to consider

AVOID THE FOUR 'F'S
Guard against the common limbo-state impulses of Freeze, Fear, Fight and Flail.

- Tell everyone you're "looking"

Protecting your interests and getting "out there" will allow you to feel productive and proactive. You will be relieved by others' sympathy and supported by their shared stories, offers to tell you about leads, and lists of recruiters for you to contact.

Then you will wait. Time will pass. Little progress may happen, and you optimism may dim as you become frustrated and concerned. Instead, spotlight this: your "failed" efforts are not about your failure: You simply need to expand your repertoire of transition techniques.

Career transitions in the twentieth century focused on replacing the lost position. Executives built a career "ladder" upon which they climbed higher and higher to more money, power and impact. Face-to-face networking, responding to ads and working with recruiters to fill openings were the main sources of opportunity then.

The Post-Millennium Workplace requires creativity, individual initiative and the ability to generate your own opportunities and find the vehicles to fund them. You will get the quickest (and most interesting) results by changing your thought process. You have substantial opportunity to re-engineer yourself into a "Portable Executive," one who creates opportunities based on worth, personal satisfaction, and available relationships and resources.*

Within the new workplace, you are more directly linked than ever to organizations that need your expertise. The trick to standing out in this supply and demand environment is to identify previously undiscovered opportunities to contribute, and then assess and negotiate your worth to these potential "buyers" of your skills and services. While there still will be positions to fill in the Post-Millennium Workplace, your greatest opportunities may be those you create, propose and drive.

See our second guide, "Portable Executive," to further explore this principle.

If you had a long career as a corporate executive, you likely thought of yourself in "WE" mode—you were one with the company. Now, the opportunity has arisen to see yourself in the "I" mode, by crafting a self-directed career strategy that supports work continuity regardless of whether you remain an employed executive or decide to strike out as a free agent, thought leader or agent of change.

"I" mode won't require a massive reinvention. Based on your executive exerience to date, you already possess the skills to present yourself in the first person...maybe for the first time in your career.

Assess and Position Yourself for the Post-Millennium Workplace

TWENTIETH CENTURY ORGANIZATION-CENTRIC CAREER	TWENTY-FIRST CENTURY SELF-MANAGED CAREER
Branding	Professional Trademark: Your Clearly Defined, Valuable Expertise
Company Culture and Image	Knowledge of (and Belief in) Your Value
Market Research	Research, Trend Spotting, Ongoing Self-Marketing
Organization's Marketing Plan	Your Identification of Potential Internal and External "Customers"
Divisional Marketing Strategy	Personal Go-To Market Strategy
Bureaucracies and Hierarchies	Project Management and Virtual Teams
Corporate-Balanced Scorecards, Performance Management	Individualized Metrics for Assessing Your Career Success and Satisfaction Factors
Company "Spirit"	Enthusiasm, Energy, Persistence and Resilience
Identity Tied to Title, Role and Organization	Identity Tied to Expertise
Worth Based on Compensation and Bonus	Worth Based on Marketability and Needed Skills/Experience
Linear Career Track	Expertise Range, Contribution and Impact

REGAIN CONTROL

"We make our fortunes and we call them fate."
— BENJAMIN DISRAELI

Transitions are a challenge for the executive used to making things happen. There's great freedom and excitement in being able to redefine your work-life—yet largely unfettered freedom requires some thoughtful management.

Embracing the fact that careers are truly fluid and that you're always in play shifts your attention from merely staying stable to giving momentum to your mobility.

FIRST:
Remember what you have always done as a leader and take control of the two areas of your life that are within your power:

- Attitudes (belief systems)
- Behavior (how you treat yourself and others)

Analyze and act on what you can actually control and what you can influence while recognizing and accepting those things beyond your control.

THEN:
Become "change ready" through a program of analysis, strategy, and motivation. Your responses to the following questionnaire can give you the foundation for developing an effective self-managed career strategy:

In the chart below on the next page, write what makes sense:
- In the center, identify what you can actually control.
- In the outer circle, list what you cannot control.
- In the middle circle, note elements currently out of your control that you may be able to alter through influence or attitude management.

Confront your sense of powerlessness in the face of transition by identifying what you can do, and focus on the functions that will bring you results.

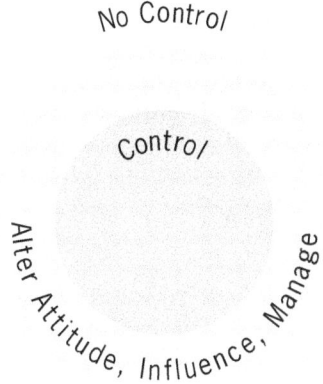

C—CONTROL: What is actually within your sphere of control? Focus on your health, thoughts, reactions, demeanor, ethics, messages, and professional comportment. Begin to gather and streamline the resources that will support your transition; these include updating your contact list, alerting close family as to the potential for a seismic change, maximizing daily exercise and keeping a more rigorous schedule of your coming weeks. Doing these things will make you feel as if you have more control, and that you're taking care of yourself.

A—ALTER: Are there ways to think about your situation that align with being change-ready and resilient? Realize that you may be able to influence that which you may not be able to change. What people, situations or messages can you manage to your advantage? Think about the image you want to portray, how you want to be thought of and remembered, how you want the media to represent you, and how your presence will affect your team and be experienced by your boss and/or board of directors. Consider ways you can influence your organization in managing challenging transitions with elegance and grace.

N—NO CONTROL: Recognize and accept that there are some situations and decisions that you cannot do anything about… and let these go. Devote your energy to what you can do, not into trying to convert final decisions, immutable conditions or intransigent people.

Transition Survival Kit

Once you've identified what you can control (and accepted that there are things you have no control over), it's time to take the next step:

- Change your route to work every Monday.
- Wear a color you've never chosen before.
- Buy new glasses (if you wear them).

Changing one small thing about yourself every week can help you practice change before you get into a rut.

Make a list of all the things you wish you could have or do if there were no barriers facing you.

Examine the list carefully. What do you find? Do you want more variety, new challenges, different people in your personal world, more fun? Is there a craft you want to pursue or a class you'd like to take?

If so, find the activity or group that will provide that experience, and do it. Be sure to write down what you did and how it felt.

Ten Tips for Dealing with Stressful Incidents and Interchanges

1. Ask yourself: "What's actually bothering me?" If you're feeling threatened, distrustful or imposed upon, look for an underlying fear, anger or hurt. What do you fear losing in this situation?
2. Consider whether this is an isolated incident, or part of a larger pattern. If it's an isolated, one-time event, you may want to hold off on a response/reaction until you gain more

information. If it's a repetitive issue, what do you think the pattern means?

3. Does the problem have roots in past history, or is it a product entirely of the present? Are you having more difficulty dealing with it because of unresolved emotions or past relationships?

4. Examine your expectations. Did you anticipate or expect a different reaction/action/or response? Is your expectation realistic considering the people/conditions?

5. Consider what you want to happen. Is there anything you can do to create this preferred outcome? What would be the consequences of your taking this action, and are you willing to accept them?

6. Go to the mat with yourself about what/whom you are trying to control. Investigate whether it is possible/useful to do so. Trying to control/change someone else's attitude/behavior/feelings is usually a fruitless effort—but perhaps you can change something about yourself.

7. Create an intellectual separation between the incident and your feelings. Ask yourself, "Is this worth doing anything about?" Sometimes taking time out to think saves lots of future work.

8. Apply the WIM test: Will It Matter in 24 seconds, 24 minutes, 24 hours? If you can delay a response or reaction for a day, sleep on it. To prepare for the wait, research your potential resources and support systems, and then write a list of steps you can initiate. Place this list aside, and then take it out after 24 hours for review.

9. Ask a confidante for his or her perspective on your planned response/action. Listen and be open to the advice.

10. Identify one small step/initiative that you can manage that will make a small change. Then build on that to larger things.

CAREER TRANSITION TOOLS

"Yesterday's thoughts have created your present. Today's thoughts are creating your future."

— JAMES NEWMAN

Playing the Odds

Mass resume mailings, trolling ads and chasing leads seem like productive activities; they allow you be "out there," letting people know you're "looking and available." It's also tempting to think that a wall of third-party recruiters and contacts who are forwarding your unsolicited resume or keeping their "eye out" for opportunities insulates you from the potential for humiliating face-to-face rejection. The irony, however, is that the proportion of rejection to activity with these methods is greater than if you utilized a more focused, targeted and personal approach.

Job Loss CPR

You've been caught up in an unexpected executive downsizing, but you've taken a deep breath and realized that it's not the end – in fact, it's a new beginning. There are three immediate steps to take:

1. Create a Reason For Leaving Statement That Has Three Parts:
- What you've accomplished in your tenure, and the impact of these achievements.
- The short and simple facts of your departure (downsizing, reorganization, change of control, financial shift) in business terms – take the high road and do not complain, criticize, or make it personal.
- What you're considering doing next (exploring opportunities in a different industry, taking some time to put a plan together, traveling, pursuing some professional projects).

2. Once That's Done, Pursue the Following:
- Plan for your financial, family, personal, physical

and professional sustenance with realistic projections that will be operational 12-24 months out.
- Create if/then scenarios, alternate plans and worst-case scenarios.
- Identify necessary lifestyle shifts, which can include increased attention to health and personal needs that may have been set aside during challenging business events.

3. Reflect Before Acting:
- Don't confuse wealth with self-worth and well-being.
- Examine whether you want to (or can) continue your career in its current form.
- Identify and work through recriminations, resentments, and regrets, lest you bring them into the search process. This is often done best with an outside counselor who is qualified to help.
- Consider how, absent of "chasing the big bucks," you want to spend your time.

Then:
Prepare to launch yourself back into the game—with careful planning and forethought to make the day-to-day transition run more smoothly:

- Behave in a transition as you do every day at work: Take charge, make a plan, engage stake-holders, have alternative paths, create backup and worst-case scenarios, and gather your resources—personal, professional and financial.
- Prepare for change by keeping track of your satisfaction, happiness factors, strengths and successes in real time.
- Keep a Transition Record of your high points and things you've learned, the people who've been helpful, and the new contacts you've made. Review this list regularly to identify themes and areas to explore or build upon, as well as ways to follow up.
- Stay connected and practice relationship quid pro

TAKE CARE OF YOURSELF
Keep fueled by getting enough sleep, eating properly and exercising.

Surround yourself with people you can count on and who care for you. Tell them what you need.

Set daily and weekly goals for getting things done. William James said that motivation follows action, not the other way around.

quo. Make this a habit even when caught up in daily demands. Keep up with it and it will not become an onerous task.

- Inoculate yourself against merging your identity and self-worth with your most recent position, your title and organizational affiliation. While these are important background facts, they don't define your future parameters.
- Be open, curious and inclusive in the exploratory stages. Avoid the temptation to eliminate options precipitously. Remember, you cannot turn down a job that hasn't been offered.
- Know when to let go of ideas, titles and goals in light of the Post-Millennium shifts in the world of work.
- Manage your advisers: Let your sponsors, mentors and resources know what you like, want and can do on an ongoing basis. Seek out and offer help, especially when you are not "needy." Make this a habit.
- Leaders thrive on identifying and fixing problems. Shift to building on what is solid, constructive and going well.
- Rise above defeat and disappointment: See every problem or mistake as an opportunity to learn and share what you've learned.
- Make it visual: Purchase a planning board for pictures, diagrams and papers detailing your quest.
- Reinforce the positive every day, both to others and (especially) within your own mind.

Manage Your Public with an Elegant Message

So now your transition is firmly underway, and you're surviving, feeling in control and ready to interact professionally.

Time to create a strategy to communicate. It's the first step to influencing others' views and gaining their support for your plans.

The goal during your time of uncertainty and planning is to manage others' desire to offer their advice, assistance, and support.

- Control Your Message (Be positive, exploratory, informative, inspirational and open; focus on what you have to offer—telling what you have to sell, rather than what you've lost/left.)
- Prepare Your Listener (During the conversation, move quickly away from sympathy, gossip and concern; guide the talk toward opportunities, openings, idea generation, expanding options, positioning, understanding your goals and what you're excited about doing next.)
- Realize and Accept that there are certain details you cannot control, such as prejudices, others' attitudes about job loss and job search, unhelpful offers to "keep an eye out for you."
- Be Conscious (Well-rehearsed "scripts" and elevator speeches can be undermined by any underlying disbelief on your part. Work through your self-consciousness, self-doubts and self-abasement before giving your "pitch." Make what you say real, exciting, energetic...and simple.)
- Create Dialogues (It's not necessary to "sell" yourself in every encounter. Ask questions, show interest, elicit information, and offer advice and assistance.)

Putting your message in play will help you regain a sense of dignity and worth. It'll give your next few steps a sense of much-needed momentum, and it'll allow you to create a transition team of supporters, advisers, connectors, informants and mentors to support you in the near future.

Perhaps the most important part of the strategy: Portray yourself to others as someone who's Leaving Happy.

IN-CONTROL TRANSITION MESSAGING

Channel your emotions into the following, productive messages:

SAY THIS	INSTEAD OF
I'm considering my next career step.	I've just been fired.
I'm putting a plan together and would like to share it with you when I am ready.	If you hear of a job, please let me know.
I'd like to share some ideas about this industry's future trends and needs; your perspectives will be very helpful as I position myself and make decisions about the future.	I really need some information and advice.
I'm taking time to assess my interests, expertise, needs and supportive environments.	I'm just focusing on getting a new position.
I take care of myself by going to the gym, investing in a hobby, being with friends/family and having some fun.	I've fired myself by not caring about my personal needs.
These are alternatives I'm exploring for feedback and input.	I'm waiting for openings and asking what's out there.
I prepare and plan my communications and messages as I would any business meeting.	I wing it.
Plant seeds	Sell myself
Act	Wait
I inspire people with what I have to offer and am excited about doing.	I "hit" on business contacts, some of whom I have not spoken with in years, to give me leads, contacts and opportunities.

Chase Leads and You'll Get Seduced

Very few people wake up in the morning and say "Oh good, I can look for work today!" So it's natural that you'd be tempted to respond to any job opening that comes your way via a recruiter or ad. Even if the position is too junior, too boring, requires relocating, or is simply something you don't want to do anymore, you may choose to pursue it anyway, in spite of your resolve to control your career identity and define yourself professionally.

There's nothing wrong with that, as long as you keep your expectations and time-expense realistic. Remember, that job opening may very well be real, but a few facts need to be kept in mind:

- Very likely there is a lot of competition for it.
- There may be a problem related to the position.
- It may not be a good fit for you.
- There already may be an internal candidate chosen.
- The employer may be "fishing"—and not really looking.
- They may never respond to you.
- You could end up in a waiting state when you could be out there pursuing your destiny.

Granted, the position could be the right fit, and you might land happily (for now). Even so, you'll want to analyze the situation through the following filters:

- Will I be expanding my expertise?
- Will this position support my reputation?
- Will it broaden my visibility?
- Will it support my career focus, so that I can Leave Happy and transition with satisfaction?

If you can answer the above points with an unqualified "yes," then it could be productive to send your resume. Should the situation pan out, and you elect to take the job, you'll then be in a far better position vis-à-vis your career than if you simply grabbed at the first semi-decent thing that came along. You'll have used your resume in the name of Work Continuity, as opposed to the pursuit of Job Security.

Post-Millennium Networking

The average elevator ride takes less than 60 seconds, just enough time for you to deliver a "news flash" to a fellow passenger. You should take your cue from that and be prepared to deliver the latest on your job/career in under a minute.

It's all about speed these days. Traditional exploratory networking and broad information meetings (often undefined and schmoozy), once accepted and welcome professional habits, are increasingly viewed as annoying and overly time-consuming. In the current reality, those old-school methods are often trumped by the following:

- Quick Phone Catch-Ups
- Focused Conversations
- Video Conferences
- Email
- Twitter/Yammer
- Social and Business Networking Sites
- Search Engines

When networking lunches, drinks and dinners do occur, you want to respect your contact's time by being prepared, having a purpose beyond learning about openings, and managing your expectations (ask for what he or she can give you in the way of advice, information, insights, feedback, and recommendations). While you may harbor a "rescue fantasy" in which your contact produces an opportunity for you based on a single networking meeting, it may be more realistic to see these meetings as "planting seeds," which you'll nurture into future opportunities through patience, mutuality, follow-ups, idea-sharing and a spirit of generosity.

At large networking gatherings or social and industry events, your goal is to cover as much ground as possible, briefly and with as many people as possible (whom you'll follow up with for longer discussions).

This is not the time to distribute your resume, ask for leads or conduct in-depth conversations about your search.

Remember three bywords for productive contact development:
- Give
- Nurture
- Collaborate

When approaching for the first time, connect through:
- Small world connections
- Mutual interests
- Discussing articles
- Discussing issues
- Asking opinions
- Gracious and polite exchanges

At every exchange:
- Have something to offer.
- Have something to discuss.
- Serve as a magnet for relationships—pull people together with commonality, mutual interest and mutual need.
- Make sure to give something of value in every encounter.

Exchange Techniques:
- Listening (Questions unite; answers divide)
- Likeability (Easy to be with; eating and enjoying together)
- Learning (Have something to bring to the exchange)
- Linking (Exchange energy and ideas, bring the necessary bursts of energy to a relationship)
- "Six Degrees of Separation" (Find the commonalities)

And Don't Forget...

Keep people informed:

- When they have been helpful.
- When something they've suggested worked.
- When you have a new idea.
- When you've met someone who might be interesting or helpful to them.
- When you are learning something that might interest them.
- When you can think of something that would be helpful to them.

RESUME ROULETTE

"The secret of getting ahead is getting started. The secret of getting started is breaking your complex overwhelming tasks into small manageable tasks, and then starting on the first one." — MARK TWAIN

Twentieth century career management and change was all about the beautifully crafted resume; most of us believed that a successful career or job change couldn't start without one. "Build it and they will come," we said to ourselves, echoing Kevin Costner in *Field of Dreams*.

Now it's time to think of your resume as just one (and maybe not the best or only) piece of career-making collateral, in the same way that print advertising is just one method a company can use to get its message out.

Resumes Are Useful Search Tools If:
- Your work history exactly matches the job specs.
- You want to do what you were doing before.
- You're seeking a job that builds on your career; in addition, you're highly marketable in your field, and few people out there do what you do.
- You write a resume that covers every eventuality. Or you create a carefully research-based "just for you" resume customized for each opportunity (e.g. private industry, government).
- It is a compelling self-presentation that reflects a real marketplace need, shepherded by a powerful connector who can make sure it ends up in the hands of an interested party.
- You follow up on your resume's distribution and advance the process with personal dialogue, whether or not the recipient actually has an immediate opening.

In the new workplace, your resume is best leveraged as a tool for exploring and developing your independent career, as opposed to a piece of paper you leave behind with someone who might have a job for you.

Expand Your Horizons, Post-Millennium Style

WAYS TO OPEN DOORS	LEADS TO A DEAD END
Gain input from contacts about your resume by using it as a draft for discussion.	Send out your resume to contacts to pass along or think of opportunities for you.
Ask contacts which recruiters they would use if they wanted to hire a person like you. Then ask for an introduction.	Send mass mailings to recruiters that introduce you as "available" so they can update their database.
Speak with existing contacts or targeted individuals to share your self-marketing plan (see later section) or discuss industry/professional trends related to your own expertise and goals.	Request meetings with casual acquaintances or strangers (referred by contacts) to "pick their brain" about your career options.
Explore the Internet and social/business networking sites for trends, inquiries, issues and groups that have common interests and issues. Increase your visibility and impact online.	Join LinkedIn or Facebook expecting people to contact you if they know of an opportunity or need someone like you.
Offer to help colleagues, contacts and key executives. Share your insights, ideas, and information. Be a connector, mentor and savvy resource.	Call contacts to tell them you are seeking other opportunities. Continue calling them to say you are still "looking."
Ask contacts for something they can do for you specifically, exclusive of knowing of or having a job for you.	Expect contacts to keep an eye out for your career and contact you.
Sleuth and research online and in person through opportunistic reading. Spot trends, gain access and have a point of view. Make known your desire to contribute to opportunities based on market analysis and needs identification.	Send resumes to ad postings and wait.
Create a launch pad for a new professional direction, or your own business.	Keep a narrow focus on replacing a position that no longer exists.
Design a customized presentation based on knowledge of an organization's needs, related to your expertise.	General purpose resume, with the reader left to figure out the fit.
Be a key opinion leader in your field and share ideas, insights and trends.	Ask others to tell you which direction to pursue based on your resume.
Increase your visibility: join boards, be active in your community, volunteer, take or teach a class, write a white paper/article/blog.	Spend most of your time searching online ads and pursuing recruiters.
Control the follow-up.	Wait for a response.

ALTERNATIVES TO RESUMES

As long as you're using that resume in non-standard (i.e., Post-Millennium Workplace) ways, why not consider some other ways to demonstrate your experience and abilities?

Biography

Although many executives never consider writing one, a professional biography that demonstrates your uniqueness can become one of the more versatile tools at your disposal. It's useful for introducing yourself to new clients and business partners, and it also makes an easy handout for media interviewers, a company, social/professional networking or a personal Web site.

Keep it short and incisive. A length of one page is ideal. Most biographies tend to be written in the third person. Include the following details:

- Expertise and range of experience (your trademark)
- Organizations for which you've worked
- Books/articles/papers you've published
- Boards on which you've served
- Educational background
- Notable media appearances—as long as they've been positive
- Awards won

Online Profile

Nowadays, many executives have embraced LinkedIn (linkedin.com) and even sites such as Facebook (facebook.com) as portals for broadcasting their message to the world. If you decide to go this route (and there's no reason why you shouldn't), keep in mind:

- **Keep It Short.** People tend to scan—as opposed to read—what they see online. When listing your accomplishments and education, keep things concise.
- **Keep It Professional.** When it comes to online, you never know who'll be reading your site. When

crafting your profile, imagine your CEO—or one of your parents—is looking over your shoulder.

- **Keep It True.** People reinvent themselves online all the time. Resist the impulse to fudge your entries—you never know who might call you on it later.

Fact Sheet + Detail Sheet

Similar to a deal sheet format, think of this as a stripped-down version of your professional resume—a short, two-page document that briefly gives your work history and background on the first page, and your achievements on the second. Select only those achievements that will support your career marketability and represent your future professional goals. State what you did (the "what") and the impact/results (the "so what?"), if the latter is quantifiable.

Capabilities Portfolio

This resume alternative can be offered either in traditional paper mode, or crafted as a PowerPoint or Web presentation; the Web is more mobile, and a Web-based work can be virtually presented to distant potential clients. Here, brief (one- to two-page) profiles detail your past projects and accomplishments; with a Web version of the portfolio, you should add links to relevant sites.

The Self-Marketing Plan

The Plan is used to outline your career management/change strategy. This is a growing, changing and iterative process that can be used as an assessment, compass and talking tool, as well as a guide for your career-management process. You will find that you will use this methodology many times in the future as you continue to transition.

The Plan's six elements are:

- **Focus**
  Describe your functional area (not job title), such as operations, marketing, human resources, etc. that represents you in the marketplace.

- **Areas of Expertise**
  What functions do you want to perform? What are the accomplishments that support those functions? What benefits do you uniquely bring to those functions?
- **Resources**
  List those people who can assist you in planning your self-marketing agenda and meeting the right contacts.
- **Target Market**
  Analyze which industries you will approach in your job search. Begin broadly, and narrow your scope based on preferred work environments, areas of interest, and personal values.
- **Representative Companies**
  Research the companies in your chosen industry for the ones whose values and plans match yours; consider how your abilities and skills are relevant to those companies' needs.
- **Situations Of Particular Interest**
  Once you've identified the characteristics of organizations that can be of potential interest, articulate situations in which you could see yourself excelling.

Then, the Plan's assessment and planning tools ask you to identify:

- **Options And Odds**
  Once you have a clearer picture of the places and positions you wish to pursue, create a list in which you prioritize your options based on their realistic potential for work within your time frame. Ideally, you should have a total list of 50-60 contacts you can approach and 6-10 options to pursue at any one time.
- **Action Plan**
  Once you have your focus, target market, representative companies and contact sources, schedule a campaign plan that allows you to balance meetings, schedule adequate follow-up and research time, and maintain your life-balance.

CONCLUSION: HAPPY TRANSITIONS IN THE POST-MILLENNIUM WORKPLACE

"A person is a success if they get up in the morning and gets [sic] to bed at night and in between does what he wants to do." —BOB DYLAN

Like many executives, you may start out defining yourself by your work and your organization. Your social support systems and stature may also be linked to your career. Work is a way for you to express and develop your expertise, and serves as a vehicle for your legacy.

So when the moment comes for your transition (one in which you continue to be your best and most productive self, without your previous work to psychologically buttress you), it will take a little planning to Leave Happy.

In order to keep in mind that you exist beyond your title, salary and organizational affiliation, it will help to develop what we'll call "transitional objects" to support your inner needs through this period:

- **Identity** (a sense of self)
  You may have gotten in the habit of defining yourself by what you do and where you do it. Instead, focus on who you are as a person; disengage your individual sense of self from what you do professionally. What do you stand for, what's important to you, and what engages you the most? What five adjectives would you choose to describe yourself? Ask others to help you with this question. You may be surprised at what they say.

- **Meaning/Purpose** (a sense of mission)
  Studies of people who survive disruptive change show that one of the three critical survival factors is a sense of commitment. What do you care deeply about, and how do you want to contribute to your world? Knowing the answers can imbue your life with a vitally important sense of mission.

- **Belonging** (a sense of place)
  Do you see your work as your family, society, structure or support system? If you were to leave your current workplace or change careers/retire, how would you connect with the larger world? What kinds of people do you like to be around? Consider ways you can engage with professional organizations, public service, family, friends, spiritual organizations and avocations that expand your ability to connect.

- **Legacy** (how you will be remembered)
  Imagine you're being toasted at an event celebrating your character, success, qualifications and achievements. What would you wish was said about you? List the qualities, activities, affiliations and achievements by which you want to be known.

Keeping focused on what matters to you and what makes you a unique individual will keep you engaged, connected, committed and motivated when the time comes to disconnect from your old support system and routine. Such soul-searching will positively influence your future choices and make you more interesting and authentic with others.

Self-Sacrifice Is Self-Destructive

All of us carry an informal transaction account in our heads. In this mental ledger, we keep track of whom we've done favors for, and who's done favors for us. These accounts work best when they're balanced; but when one person gives or takes too much, that building sense of obligation creates resentment: We feel that we "owe" someone, or that he or she has taken too much from us.

Reciprocity and elegance always trump obligation and resentment. It's not worth killing yourself to give; and whenever you take, remember to give back, even in a small way. Take the example of Jacqueline Kennedy, who was much admired for her handwritten letters of appreciation, recognition, congratulations, and condolences—even by hardnosed political figures such as Nikita Khrushchev, to whom she sent a note after JFK's assassination thanking him for working so well with her husband.

During your transition period, it's more important than ever to stay aware of what you've done for people, and who's done what for you. When things are up in the air, being able to rely on someone on short notice is vital. If your personal resources are limited, keeping accurate stock of what you're giving is equally important, so you don't overextend yourself to others while ignoring your own health or professional needs.

ELEGANT EXECUTIVE TRANSITION REMINDERS

Remember: These are times of seismic change, a true period of spiritual, environmental, cultural and information revolution. Prospering within this context will take a radically different mindset, one that acknowledges that your career is no longer governed predominantly by benign or malevolent external forces: It's up to you to Leave (as well as work and arrive) Happy.

TRY THIS	INSTEAD OF
Think about your most marketable attributes and potential outlets for them.	Write and broadly distribute your resume.
Link with sources to connect with whoever needs what you have to offer.	Network indiscriminately
Consider multiple ways to work.	Think of where you can find jobs.
Go for the opportunity to grow, contribute and expand your visibility.	Go after the big bucks regardless of intrinsic interest.
Consider what matters to you in the work you do, people you associate with, the environment in which you thrive.	Think only about position, prestige and power.
Appreciate the career you've had, and articulate the portable expertise you've gained and contributions made.	Complain and criticize
Write a self-marketing plan.	Answer job ads and chase leads
Identify emerging industries and alternative or interim ways to work.	Resent the change in your status.
Use multiple models of how to work.	Use one job-search model.
Seek growing and emerging markets.	Focus on shrinking and mature markets.
Expand ideas ("I am investigating alternatives to consider.")	Eliminate options ("I don't want to do that.")
Demonstrate positive resilience.	Express recriminations, resentments and regret.

Dr. Karen Otazo has been a global executive coach and mentor for executives in transnational companies worldwide for more than 25 years. Her second book, The Truth About Being a Leader *(2007), was recognized as one of the Top Five Best Business Books for 2007 by* Strategy and Business.

Dr. Otazo's experience makes her uniquely equipped to work with executives connecting cultures in global corporations, national subsidiaries, international ventures and strategic alliances.

She sits on the boards of Vital Voices Global Partnership, Citizens for Affordable Energy and Best Partners. Karen is a fellow of SoL, the Society for Organizational Learning, an international learning community dedicated to sustainable business.

www.global-leadership-network.com

Sheryl Spanier is a thought leader, media contributor and master practitioner of Executive Career Management who is sought out to coach and advise international leaders and their teams. After working as a consultant and market leader for four premier career management companies, she started her own firm in 2004. With more than 25 years in the field, Spanier combines empathy and pragmatism to coach clients in maximizing the interpersonal side of their business strategies and to lead individual and organizational change.

She is a member of Phi Beta Kappa, a founding member of the Association for Career Professionals International and is certified as a Fellow by the Institute for Career Certification International.

www.sherylspanier.com

www.ingramcontent.com/pod-product-compliance
Lightning Source LLC
Chambersburg PA
CBHW051305170526
45165CB00004B/1853